anything is GOOD if it's made of CHOCOLATE.
JO BRAND

forget love — I'd rather fall in CHOCO- LATE!

SANDRA J. DYKES

let's face it,

a nice creamy chocolate **CAKE**

does a lot for a lot of **PEOPLE;**

it does for **ME.**

AUDREY HEPBURN

IF THERE'S NO CHOCOLATE IN HEAVEN, I'M NOT GOING.

Jane Seabrook

WHAT YOU see before you, my friend, IS THE RESULT OF a LIFETIME of chocolate.

KATHARINE HEPBURN

Chocolate SYMBOLIZES, as does no other food, LUXURY, COMFORT, SENSUALITY, GRATIFICATION, AND LOVE. *Karl Petzke*

very now and then,
'll run into someone
ho claims not to like
chocolate,
nd while we live
n a country where
veryone has the right
o eat what
hey want,

I want to say for
the record that I
don't trust
these people...

STEVE ALMOND

chocolate
is a
permanent
thing.

Milton S. Hershey